WHAT ABOUT OTHER RELIGIONS?

What About Other Religions?

NICKY GUMBEL

KINGSWAY PUBLICATIONS
EASTBOURNE

ISBN 0 85476 863 7

Illustrations by Charlie Mackesy

Published by
KINGSWAY COMMUNICATIONS LTD
Lottbridge Drove, Eastbourne, BN23 6NT, England.
Email: books@kingsway.co.uk

Print production for the publishers by
Bookprint Creative Services, P.O. Box 827, BN21 3YJ, England.
Printed in Great Britain.

Contents

What About Other Religions?

The impression is often given that Christianity is dying out in the United Kingdom. It is said that we live in a pluralist society in which other religions are gradually taking over. Actually, this impression of a multi-faith Britain is misleading. Only 2.5 per cent of the population are adherents of other faiths. Some 10 per cent go to Christian churches and 80 per cent would probably go to a Christian church if they went anywhere.

Worldwide, Christianity is by far the largest 'religion'. According to the *Encyclopedia Britannica*, it has 1,900 million adherents, amounting to 34 per cent of the world population. There are 880 million Muslims, 663 million Hindus and 311 million Buddhists, in addition to many other smaller groupings such as Jews, Sikhs, Bahais and tribal religions. Atheists amount to a mere 4.5 per cent of the world population.

Even if Christianity predominates, we still need to face the question of what Christians say about other religions. Modern communications have made us all increasingly aware of other faiths. We are brought into contact with many religions on television and radio, as well as through personal contact in the classroom, neighbourhood, work and social activities. What are we to say about these other religions?

IS JESUS THE ONLY WAY TO GOD?

The answer of the New Testament is an emphatic 'Yes'.

Jesus himself said, 'I am the way and the truth and the life. No-one comes to the Father except through me' (John 14:6). He claimed to be the way to God and, indeed, the only way. The columnist Bernard Levin makes the point that Jesus used unequivocal language:

> I take it that a religion which claims to be following the truth, the whole truth and nothing but the truth must, even if only by a process of elimination, think that the other religions are, for all their holiness and worship, mistaken. I, of all people, should not bandy scripture with experts, but in these ecumenical days it is surely reasonable to ask Christianity what its founder meant when he said, 'None shall come to the Father but by me.' I do not offer those words to give offence, but many a devout Christian is worried by them, and many a bishop, opening his heart to other faiths, must be hard put to it to provide an answer. I doubt if you will get a very convincing answer anywhere, bishop or no bishop.[1]

When Peter and John healed the crippled man outside the temple, a large crowd gathered. Peter proclaimed Jesus as the 'author of life' who had been crucified but was now resurrected and glorified. They were arrested and put on trial and asked 'by what power' the crippled man had been healed. Peter, 'filled with the Holy Spirit', replied that it was 'by the name of Jesus Christ of Nazareth' and that 'salvation is found in no-one else, for there is no other name under heaven given to people by which we must be saved' (Acts 4:12).

Peter, inspired by the Holy Spirit, is unequivocal. Jesus is the only name that can save. His answer is consistent with the rest of the New Testament. St Paul is equally emphatic: 'For there is one God and one mediator between God and human beings, Christ Jesus, himself human' (1 Timothy 2:5). So the writer of Hebrews warns us that there is no other means of escape except through Jesus Christ: 'How shall we escape if we ignore such a great salvation?' (Hebrews 2:3).

What makes Jesus unique? First, he is unique in his qualification. Peter proclaimed him as the 'Holy and Righteous One' (Acts 3:14), the 'author of life' (v 15). He is the one the prophets foretold (v 18). He is the 'Christ' (v 20). He is the one whom the early church worshipped as God.

This sets him apart from the leaders of the other great world religions. Muslims do not like being described as Muhammadans because they do not worship Muhammad. 'No one in the Islamic world has ever dreamed of according to him divine honours – he would have been the first to reject any such suggestion as blasphemy.'[2] It is not clear

9

whether Buddha believed in the existence of God as such. 'Early or classical Buddhism had no god.'[3]

Secondly, Jesus is unique in his achievement. As Peter asserts, 'salvation is found in no-one else, for there is no other name under heaven given to people by which we must be saved' (Acts 4:12). We all need a saviour because we have all sinned and we cannot save ourselves from the results of sin. None of the other great religions even claims to have a saviour. 'The English Buddhist, Maurice Walsh, pointed out that the Buddhist view of Buddha is very different from the Christian view of Christ. He stressed that the Buddha is thought of as a Teacher – not as a Saviour.'[4] Likewise, Muhammad is regarded as a prophet – not as a saviour. In Islam, sinners will face judgement without forgiveness.

By contrast, Jesus is the one who brings salvation. He saves us from our guilt, he saves us from the addictive power of sin and he saves us from the judgement we all deserve.

Thirdly, Jesus is unique in his resurrection. Peter described him as the one 'whom God raised from the dead' (Acts 4:10). The resurrection is a unique event in the history of the world.

The Pali Canon of Buddhism records the great entrance of . . . the Buddha into Nirvana . . . but there is no suggestion that the Buddha will continue to be present with his followers after his death; the *dhamma*, the teaching, will take his place and will be their guide . . . the exact date of the death of the prophet Muhammad is known. No one has ever supposed that he survived the accident of physical death.[5]

By contrast, the resurrection of Jesus lies at the heart of the Christian faith. Jesus Christ is alive today. We can know him. We cannot know Buddha or Muhammad. Jesus, the unique Son of God, the unique Saviour, the one uniquely raised from the dead, is the only way to God. If Jesus is the only way to God, this immediately raises two further questions: first, 'What do we say about other religions?' Secondly, 'What about those who have never heard about Jesus?'

WHAT DO WE SAY ABOUT OTHER RELIGIONS?

The fact that Jesus is the only way to God does not mean that we simply write off all other religions as misguided or demonic. Jesus said, 'I am the truth.' In him, ultimate truth is to be found and he is the standard by which all truth claims are to be tested. But this does not mean that parts of the truth cannot be found in other religions. Indeed, we would expect to find truth in other religions for at least three reasons.

First, although God's revelation of himself in Jesus, witnessed to in Scripture, is unique and final, God has partially revealed himself in creation. 'The heavens declare the glory of God; the skies proclaim the work of his hands' (Psalm 19:1). The pinnacle of his creation is human life. As Sir Isaac Newton, the brilliant physicist and mathematician, said, 'In the absence of any other proof, the thumb alone would convince me of God's existence.'

11

Therefore, the psalmist says, only a fool can claim that 'there is no God' (Psalm 14:1; 53:1) 'For since the creation of the world God's invisible qualities – his eternal power and divine nature – have been clearly seen, being understood from what has been made, so that they are without excuse' (Romans 1:20). From creation, it is possible for men and women to find out the truth about God's existence and gain an insight into his character: his power and his glory. The evidence provided by creation is available to all, and could therefore be found in other religions.

Secondly, human beings are made in the image of God and God has given us a conscience with which to distinguish right and wrong. As Paul put it, 'Indeed, when Gentiles, who do not have the law, do by nature things required by the law . . . they show that the requirements of the law are written on their hearts, their consciences also bearing witness, and their thoughts now accusing, now even defending them' (Romans 2:14–15). Thus, it is not surprising that the essence of 'the golden rule' ('Do to others what you would have them do to you' – Matthew 7:12) is contained in almost every religion from Confucius (551–479 BC) onwards.

Thirdly, in every heart there is a hunger for God. God has 'set eternity in the human heart' (Ecclesiastes 3:11). Deep down no one is satisfied by materialism; we know there is more to life. There is a God-shaped gap in the heart of every human being. This hunger drives us to search for God. It is one of the explanations as to why there are so few atheists in the world and why so many seek earnestly after God.

It is understandable then that we find good in many religions. Of course, we will be challenged as Christians by aspects of the lives of adherents to other religions, for example, their commitment, their devotion or their dedication to what they believe.

It also explains why there is often a certain continuity for those who become Christians from other faiths. Bishop Lesslie Newbigin, who was a bishop in South India for forty years, spoke of

> an element of continuity which is confirmed in the experience of many who have become converts to Christianity from other religions. Even though this conversion involves a radical discontinuity, yet there is often the strong conviction afterwards that it was the living and true God who was dealing with them in the days of their pre-Christian wrestlings.[6]

Nevertheless, it is illogical to assert that all religions are equally true or that all religions lead to God. The theologian, Alister McGrath, points out that some world religions are avowedly non-theistic and that 'a religion can hardly lead to God if it explicitly denies the existence of a god or any gods'.[7] Equally, it is absurd to suggest that a religion which asserts that there is a god and one that asserts there is no god are both equally true. Since there are contradictions between the religions, there must be error somewhere. Indeed, we would expect to find error in other religions.

We are all fallen human beings (Christian and non-Christian alike), and none of us can find God by ourselves. But God has revealed himself in the person of Jesus who is 'the truth'. Only in Jesus Christ do we find infallible truth. That is not to say that Christians are infallible, or that our understanding of the truth is infallible, but that God's revelation in Jesus Christ is infallible. He is the standard by which all truth claims must be examined.

By putting other religions alongside God's revelation in Jesus Christ, we see that they contain both truth and error. There is a dark side to other religions. There may be a dark side to the way some people use Christianity, but there is no dark side to God's revelation in Jesus Christ.

This is not arrogant, narrow minded or illiberal, as some would suggest. As C. S. Lewis wrote:

> If you are a Christian you do not have to believe that all the other religions are simply wrong all through. If you are an atheist you do have to believe that the main point in all the religions of the whole world is simply one huge mistake. If you are a Christian, you are free to think that all those religions, even the queerest ones, contain at least some hint of the truth. When I was an atheist I had to try to persuade myself that most of the human race have always been wrong about the question that mattered to them most; when I became a Christian I was

14

able to take a more liberal view. But, of course, being a Christian does mean thinking that where Christianity differs from other religions, Christianity is right and they are wrong. As in arithmetic – there is only one right answer to a sum, and all other answers are wrong; but some of the wrong answers are much nearer being right than others.[8]

WHAT ABOUT THOSE WHO HAVE NEVER HEARD ABOUT JESUS?

This is the second question raised by the New Testament's claim that there is no other way to God. If we can only be saved through Jesus, are all the rest damned? If so, is that not unjust? In answering these questions I usually try to make the following five points.

First, the Bible is a practical book, not a philosophical one. It does not answer hypothetical questions directly. This question can only ever be hypothetical, since it can only be asked by someone who has heard about Jesus.

Secondly, we can be sure that God will be just. When Abraham asked the rhetorical question, 'Will not the Judge of all the earth do right?' (Genesis 18:25), he clearly expected the answer, 'Yes, of course he will.' We need not fear that God will be unjust. He will be more just than we are, not less. On Judgement Day, every right-thinking person will say of God's judgement: 'That is completely just.'

Thirdly, what we do know is that no one will be saved by their religion. We are saved by God's undeserved love through faith in Jesus Christ (Ephesians 2:8). He died for us

15

so that we can be forgiven. We receive salvation when we accept the gift by faith.

Fourthly, it is important to note that it is possible to be saved by grace, through faith, even if someone has never heard of Jesus. 'Abraham believed God, and it was credited to him as righteousness' (Romans 4:3). Paul tells us that David also speaks of 'the blessedness of the man to whom God credits righteousness apart from works' (Romans 4:6). This is possible because the cross is effective for all those who lived before as well as after Jesus. Abraham and David were forgiven because of what Jesus was to do for them on the cross. They did not have the advantage that we have of knowing how it is possible to be forgiven. They did not have the assurance that we have as a result of knowing about 'Jesus Christ and him crucified' (1 Corinthians 2:2). Nevertheless, Paul tells us that they were justified by faith.

In the same way, the person who lived at the time of Jesus or after him would be justified by faith – even if they had not heard about him. So Jesus tells us in the parable of the Pharisee and the tax collector that the tax collector who said, 'God, have mercy on me, a sinner,' went home justified before God (Luke 18:9–14). Surely the same is true for anyone today who has not heard of Jesus but did what the tax collector did.

So the essential elements would seem to be a God-given sense of sin or need, and a self-abandonment to God's mercy. If a man of whom this is true subsequently hears and understands the gospel, then I myself believe that he would be among the company of those, whom one does sometimes meet on the mission field, who welcome and accept it at once, saying (in effect): 'This is what I have been waiting for all these years. Why didn't you come and tell me before?' And if he never hears the gospel here on earth, then I suppose that he will wake up, as it were, on the other side of the grave to worship the One in whom, without understanding it at the time, he had found the mercy of God.[9]

Fifthly, as John Stott points out, there are biblical grounds for great optimism. Abraham's descendants (spiritual as well as physical) will be 'as numerous as the stars in the sky and as the sand on the seashore' (Genesis 22:17). 'In the same vein we seem to be assured by Paul that many more people will be saved than lost because Christ's work in causing salvation will be more successful than Adam's in causing ruin and because God's grace in bringing life will overflow "much more" than Adam's trespass in bringing death.'[10] (See Romans 5:2.)

If that is the case, why should we bother to tell others about Jesus? First, because the glory of Jesus Christ is at stake. Secondly, because Jesus commanded us to go into all the world and tell the good news. Thirdly, because without knowing about Jesus no one could have the assurance of forgiveness and the abundant life he offers both in this life and in the life to come. For Jesus is not only the way and the truth, he is also 'the life'.

WHAT SHOULD WE DO?

We have no excuse. No one who has read this booklet will ever be able to say, 'I never heard about Jesus.' So also we

17

have no other escape. As the writer of Hebrews warns us all, 'How shall we escape if we ignore such a great salvation?' (Hebrews 2:3).

As far as others are concerned, our task is to tell them the good news about Jesus. If the early Christians had not been willing to tell the good news about Jesus to those who already had a religion of their own, Christianity would have died in a generation.

> The Christian points to the one Lord Jesus Christ as the Lord of all men . . . the Church does not apologise for the fact that it wants all men to know Jesus Christ and to follow him. Its very calling is to proclaim the Gospel to the ends of the earth. It cannot make any restrictions in this respect. Whether people have a high, a low or a primitive religion, whether they have sublime ideals or a defective morality makes no fundamental difference in this respect. All must hear the Gospel.[11]

Of course we need to be humble and sensitive. Christians are no better than those of other religions or those of no religion. We are all in the same boat; we all need a saviour and there is no room for arrogance.

Secondly, we need to be positive. Peter in Acts 4 did not attack other faiths. He preached the good news about Jesus.

Thirdly, we need to be respectful. We need to respect everyone as those who were made in the image of God – whether they are Christians or not.

Finally, we need to be courageous. The early Christians were unashamed witnesses to Jesus. Their message was unpopular and it got them into trouble. But they did not stop. We need to do the same in an age when tolerance, not truth, is the order of the day.

It is important to remember that 'the pluralism of the first and second centuries AD was the greatest in extent and intensity the world has ever seen'. But, as Michael Green goes on to say, 'Far from closing our options, pluralism allows us to proclaim an undiluted gospel in the public square and in the supermarket of faiths, allowing others the same right. Let the truth prevail and let craven silence be banished.'[12]

FOR FURTHER READING

Stephen Neill, *The Supremacy of Jesus* (Hodder & Stoughton, 1984).
Lesslie Newbigin, *The Gospel in a Pluralist Society* (SPCK, 1989).
John Stott, *The Contemporary Christian* (IVP, 1992), chapter 18.

NOTES

1. Bernard Levin, *The Times* (27th January 1992).
2. Stephen Neill, *The Supremacy of Jesus* (Hodder & Stoughton, 1984), p82.
3. John Stott, *The Contemporary Christian* (IVP, 1992), p308.
4. John Young, *The Case Against Christ* (Hodder & Stoughton, 1986), p152.
5. Stephen Neill, *op cit*, p82.
6. Lesslie Newbigin, *The Finality of Christ* (John Knox Press, 1969), p59.
7. Alister McGrath, *Bridgebuilding* (IVP, 1992), p151.
8. C. S. Lewis, *Mere Christianity* (Fount, 1952), p39.
9. J. N. D. Anderson, *Christianity and Comparative Religion* (IVP, 1970), p105.
10. John Stott, *op cit*, p319.
11. Lesslie Newbigin, *op cit*, p59.
12. Michael Green, *Evangelism through the Local Church* (Hodder & Stoughton, 1990) p75.

Alpha

This book is an Alpha resource. The Alpha course is a practical introduction to the Christian faith initiated by Holy Trinity Brompton in London, and now being run by thousands of churches throughout the UK as well as overseas.

For more information on Alpha, and details of tapes, videos and training manuals, contact the Alpha office, Holy Trinity Brompton on 0207 581 8255, (home page: http://www.alpha.org.uk), or STL, PO Box 300, Kingstown Broadway, Carlisle, Cumbria CA3 0QS.

Alpha Hotline for telephone orders:
0845 7581 278 (all calls at local rate)

To order from overseas:
Tel +44 1228 512512
Fax +44 1228 514949

 Kingsway Publications

Alpha

Alpha titles available

Why Jesus? A booklet given to all participants at the start of the Alpha course. 'The clearest, best illustrated and most challenging short presentation of Jesus that I know.' – Michael Green

Why Christmas? The Christmas version of *Why Jesus?*

Questions of Life The Alpha course in book form. In fifteen compelling chapters Nicky Gumbel points the way to an authentic Christianity which is exciting and relevant to today's world.

A Life Worth Living What happens after Alpha? Based on the book of Philippians, this is an invaluable next step for those who have just completed the Alpha course, and for anyone eager to put their faith on a firm biblical footing.

Telling Others: The Alpha Initiative The theological principles and the practical details of how courses are run. Each alternate chapter consists of a testimony of someone whose life has been changed by God through an Alpha course.

Challenging Lifestyle Studies in the Sermon on the Mount showing how Jesus' teaching flies in the face of modern lifestyle and presents us with a radical alternative.

30 Days Nicky Gumbel selects thirty passages from the Old and New Testament which can be read over thirty days. It is designed for those on an Alpha course and others who are interested in beginning to explore the Bible.

The Heart of Revival Ten Bible studies based on the book of Isaiah, drawing out important truths for today by interpreting some of the teaching of the Old Testament prophet Isaiah. The book seeks to understand what revival might mean and how we can prepare to be part of it.

All titles are by Nicky Gumbel, who is on the staff of Holy Trinity Brompton

——— ❖ ———